W9-CSY-606

Creative Art & Activities

Painting

Mary Mayesky

THOMSON
DELMAR LEARNING

Australia   Canada   Mexico   Singapore   Spain   United Kingdom   United States

THOMSON

DELMAR LEARNING

Creative Art and Activities: Painting
Mary Mayesky

Vice President, Career Ed SBU:
Dawn Gerrain

Director of Editorial:
Sherry Gomoll

Acquisitions Editor:
Erin O'Connor

Developmental Editor:
Alexis Ferraro

Editorial Assistant:
Ivy Ip

Director of Production:
Wendy A. Troeger

Production Coordinator:
Nina Tucciarelli

Composition:
Stratford Publishing Services

Director of Marketing:
Donna J. Lewis

Cover Design:
Tom Cicero

Library of Congress Cataloging-in-Publication
Data

Mayesky, Mary

1-4018-3475-2

NOTICE TO THE READER

To Ann,

a dedicated mother, loving wife, and my true friend.

With love, Mary

Contents

INTRODUCTION vii

GETTING STARTED vii

Process vs. Product vii

Considering the Child vii

Using Painting Materials and Equipment vii

Gathering Materials viii

Using Food Products x

Employing Safe Materials x

Creating a Child-Friendly Environment xi

The Painting Process—Some Basics xi

Enjoying the Painting Process xiii

Exploring Finger Painting xiv

ACTIVITIES

Accordion Painting 1

Baby-Oil Painting 2

Bag Finger Painting 3

Batik Painting 4

Blow Painting 5

Bubble Painting 6

Cardboard-Brush Painting 7

Chocolate-Pudding Finger Painting 8

Cold-Cream Finger Painting 9

Comb Painting 10

Cotton-Ball Painting 11

Crayon-Resist Painting 12

Crayons and Tempera Paint Washing 13

Dipping It! 14

Dragged Abstracts 15

Eye-Dropper Painting 16

Finger Painting on Tabletops 17

Finger Painting on Wax Paper 18

Finger Painting Over Crayon 19

Finger Painting with Shaving Cream 20

Flour-and-Water Painting 21

Fold-Over Painting 22

Hide-and-Seek Painting 23

Ice-Cube Painting 24

Leaf Painting 25

Making Painted Backpacks 26

Making Stand-Up Painted Faces 27

Marble Painting 28

Newspaper Painting 29

Painting on Cardboard 30

Painting on Damp Paper 31

Painting Snow Pictures with Cotton 32

Painting through Tissue 33

Painting to Music 34

Painting with Weeds 35

Paper-Towel Painting 36

Plastic Wrap Painting 37

Pulled-String Painting 38

Q-Tip© Painting 39

Salty Painting 40

Sand Painting 41

Spatter Painting 42

Sponge Painting 43

Spray Painting 44

Tempera and White-Glue Resist Painting 45

Three-Dimensional Painting 46

Tie Dyeing 47

Tissue-Dab Painting 48

Water Painting 49

Wax-Paper Painting 50

Window Gardening 51

Windy-Day Painting 52

INDEX BY AGES **53**

Introduction

Painting comes naturally to young children. It is a way children visually communicate their ideas and feelings about themselves and their world. Painting encourages the spontaneous use of color in the joyful process of creating.

Through painting, children can express their reactions about the world as they understand it. In this way, children discover and build their own styles of expression. Each child's painting differs from another child's, just as children's appearances and personalities differ.

The activities in this book are designed for children aged 2 through 8. An icon representing a suggested age for the activity is listed at the top of each activity. However, use your knowledge of the child's abilities to guide you in choosing and using the activities in this book. Wherever appropriate, information is provided on how to adapt the activities for children over age 8.

GETTING STARTED

Process vs. Product

The focus of this book and all early childhood art activities is on the process, not the product. This means that the process of creating, not the product, is the main reason for the activity. The joys of creating, exploring materials, and discovering how things look and work are all part of the creative process. How the product looks, what it is "supposed to be," is unimportant to the child, and it should be unimportant to the adult.

Young children delight in the experience, the exploration, and the experimentation of art activities. The adult's role is to provide interesting materials and an environment that encourages children's creativity. Stand back when you are tempted to "help" children with their artwork. Instead, encourage all children to discover their own unique abilities.

Considering the Child

Young children find it hard to wait patiently to use materials in an activity. Often, the excitement of creativity and patience do not mix. In addition, it is sometimes difficult for young children to share. With young children, plan to have enough materials for each child. For example, having a paintbrush and paint for each child to use makes the process of painting more fun and relaxed for young children.

Using Painting Materials and Equipment

The most basic materials you will need for painting activities are paint, brushes, and paper. Following are some hints for each of these painting materials.

• Paint

The most basic type of paint young children use is tempera paint. It comes in dry-powder and liquid forms. With liquid tempera, water is unneeded, although liquid tempera may be diluted with water to thin paint for different activities, like crayon-resist paintings. The dry form of tempera can be made very thick or very thin, depending on the amount of water added.

Watercolor paint sets are dehydrated tempera colors in concentrated cakes. They are easy and convenient for individual or group use.

Using Paints in Cakes: Place a few drops of water on the surface of each cake to moisten the paint. Dip the paintbrush in water, and brush the surface of the moistened cake of paint to obtain smooth, creamy paint.

Using Powder (Tempera) Paint: A surprising amount of dry tempera is needed relative to the quantity of water to make rich, bright, creamy paint. For this reason, it is best to put the tempera in the container first, then add water bit by bit. Fill a container one-quarter full of dry paint. Add water slowly, stirring constantly until the paint has the consistency of thin cream. Instead of water, some teachers prefer using liquid starch (found in the grocery store in the laundry aisle), because it thickens the paint mixture. It is also helpful to add a dash of liquid detergent, which eases cleaning.

For best results, prepare paint when needed. Large amounts of paint kept over time tend to sour. Good containers for use with tempera paint include milk cartons, juice cans, coffee cans, plastic cups, and cut-down plastic bottles. See **Figure 1** for more helpful hints for storing and handling painting materials.

- **Brushes**
Large, long-handled brushes are best for young children's painting. Those with 12" handles and 3/4" bristle length are easy for young children to use. Soft, floppy, camel-hair brushes allow the children to swoop about the paper most freely. The stiff, flat kind of brush makes it harder to produce such free movements. Many watercolor paint sets come with paintbrushes designed for watercolor use.

- **Paper**
Pieces of paper measuring 12" × 18" work well for painting, as do roll paper, manila paper, newspaper, wallpaper, newsprint, and freezer paper. More details on different types of materials for painting are provided in specific activities.

- **Easels and Other Surfaces**
An ideal way for children to paint is at child-level easels, but painting can still be an enjoyable, creative experience when easels are not available. Painting can be done on a tabletop. Simply cover the area with newspapers, place a piece of paper on top, and let the painting begin! Another way to paint is to cover a wall space with a large piece of plastic. Cover the area below the plastic with newspapers Tape pieces of paper (masking tape works best) to the plastic-covered wall.

Gathering Materials

Each activity in this book includes a list of required materials. It is important to gather all materials before starting the activity with children. Children's creative experiences are easily discouraged when they must sit and wait while the adult looks for the tape, extra scissors, or colored paper. Be sure to gather the materials in a place the children can easily access.

FIGURE 1 · TIPS FOR STORING ART MATERIALS

The ways materials, supplies, and space are arranged can make or break children's and teachers' art experiences. Following are suggestions for arranging supplies for art experiences:

1. *Scissor holders*. Holders can be made from gallon milk or bleach containers. Simply punch holes in the containers and place scissors in the holes with the scissor points to the inside. Egg cartons turned upside down with slits in each mound also make excellent holders.

2. *Paint containers*. Containers can range from muffin tins and plastic egg cartons to plastic soft-drink cartons with baby food jars in them. These work especially well outdoors as well as indoors, because they are large and not easily tipped. Place one brush in each container. This prevents colors from mixing and makes cleanup easier.

3. *Crayon containers*. Juice and vegetable cans painted or covered with contact paper work very well.

4. Crayon pieces may be melted in muffin trays in a warm oven. These pieces, when cooled, are nice for rubbings or drawings. Crayola® makes a unit that is designed specifically for melting crayons safely.

5. Printing with tempera is easier if the tray is lined with a sponge or a paper towel.

6. A card file for art activities helps organize the program.

7. *Clay containers*. Airtight coffee cans and plastic food containers are excellent ways to keep clay moist and always ready for use.

8. *Paper scrap boxes*. By keeping two or more boxes of scrap paper of different sizes, children will be able to choose the size paper they want more easily.

9. Cover a wall area with pegboard and suspend heavy shopping bags or transparent plastic bags from hooks inserted in the pegboard to hold miscellaneous art supplies. Hang smocks in the same way on the pegboard (at child level, of course).

10. Use the back of a piano or bookcase to hang a shoe bag. Its pockets can hold many small items.

11. Use divided frozen food trays or a revolving lazy Susan to hold miscellaneous small items.

(From Mayesky, Mary. *Creative Activites for Young Children*, 7th ed., Clifton Park, NY: Delmar Learning.)

Using Food Products

Several activities involve the use of different kinds of foods. There are long-standing arguments for and against food use in art activities. For example, many teachers have long used potato printing as a traditional printing activity for young children. These teachers feel they are an economical way to prepare printing objects for children. Using potatoes beyond their shelf life is an alternative to throwing them away. On the other hand, many teachers feel that food is for eating and should be used for nothing else.

This book has many activities that do not use food so that there will be options for teachers who oppose food use in art activities. Also, where possible, alternatives to food items are suggested. Whatever your opinion, creativities in painting are provided for your and the children's exploration and enjoyment.

Employing Safe Materials

For all activities in this book and in any art activities for young children, be sure to use safe art supplies. Read labels on all art materials. Check for age appropriateness. The Art and Creative Materials Institute (ACMI) labels art materials AP (approved product) and CL (certified label). Products with these labels are certified safe for use by young children.

The ACMI provides an extensive list of materials and manufacturers of safe materials for all young children. This information is available on the ACMI Web site at http://www.acminet.org by writing to 715 Boylston Street, Boston, MA 02116.

Some basic safety hints for art activities are:

- Always use products that are appropriate for the child. Use nontoxic materials for children in grades six and lower.
- Never use products for skin painting or food preparation unless the products are intended for those uses.
- Do not transfer art materials to other containers. You will lose the valuable safety information that is on the product packages.
- Do not eat or drink while using art and craft materials. Wash after use. Clean yourself and your supplies.
- Be sure that your work area is well ventilated.

Following are potentially unsafe painting supplies:

- *Epoxy, instant glues, or other solvent-based glues.* Use only water-based, white glue.
- *Paints that require solvents like turpentine to clean.* Use only water-based paints.
- *Cold water or commercial dyes that contain chemical additives.* Use only natural vegetable dyes made from beets, onion skins, and so on.
- *Permanent markers.* Permanent markers may contain toxic solvents. Use only water-based markers.

Be aware of all children's allergies. Children with allergies to wheat, for example, may be irritated by the wheat paste used in papier-mâché. Children allergic to peanuts must taste nothing with peanut butter. In fact, some centers make it a rule to avoid the use of peanuts or peanut butter in food or art activities. Other art materials that may cause allergic reactions include chalk or other dusty substances, water-based clay, and any material that contains petroleum products.

Also be aware of children's habits. Some young children put everything in their mouths. (This can be the case at any age.) Others may be shy and slow to accept new materials. Use your knowledge of children's tendencies to help you plan art activities that are safe for all children.

Take the time to talk with the children about which things they may taste and which they may not. For example, when making anything mixed with glue, remind the children that glue is not to be tasted. You may find it helpful to display a sign of a large smiley face with a tongue at the end of the smile to indicate an "edible activity." Use another sign with the same smiley face but a large black X over the tongue to show a "no-taste activity."

Creating a Child-Friendly Environment

It is difficult to be creative when you have to worry about keeping yourself and your work area clean. Cover all artwork areas with newspaper. It is best to tape the paper to the work surface to avoid having paint or other materials seep through the spaces. In addition, it is much easier to pick up and throw away paint-spattered newspaper than it is to clean a tabletop.

Other coverups that work well are shower curtains and plastic tablecloths. Remember to cover the children, too! Some good child coverups are men's shirts (with the sleeves cut off), aprons, pillowcases with holes cut for the head and arms, and smocks. Some fun alternative to these are sets of old clothes or shoes that can be worn as "art clothes." These old clothes could become "art journals" as they become covered with the traces of various art projects.

Other things to have on hand while painting are paper towels or scrap paper for blotting brushes. A bucket of child-sized, moist sponges is also handy to have on hand for cleanup.

Another hint to easier cleanup after painting is to cut and laminate both sides of a posterboard that fits the painting easel. Tape the laminated posterboard over the easel so that the children can easily wipe off the paint with a damp cloth, rag, or paper towel. Such a posterboard helps children learn how to clean up, keeps the easel clean, and develops more hand-eye coordination in a fun way.

The Painting Process—Some Basics

Following are some hints for making the painting process run smoothly:

- Thicken tempera paint with liquid starch to cut down on drips.
- To help paint stick better to such slick surfaces as foil, wax paper, Styrofoam, or plastic, mix dry tempera with liquid soap.
- To keep paints smelling fresh and sweet, add a few drops of mint extract or oil of wintergreen or cloves, which are available in the spices section of the grocery store.
- Lay paintings horizontally to dry before stacking. An unused floor space along the wall works well for this purpose, or use a stacking rack as **Figure 2** illustrates. See **Figure 3** for ideas on stretching painting-budget dollars.

FIGURE 2 · SOME HELPFUL HINTS FOR STORING AND HANDLING PAINTING MATERIALS

Art Tool Holder
Heavy paper, folded several times, will make a holder that keeps tools from rolling.

Drying Rack
Drying racks for wet artwork are ideal when space is at a premium. A number of wooden sticks of the same size, tacked or stapled to pieces of corrugated cardboard of the same size, make a drying rack. When pieces of wood are unavailable, substitute two, three, or four pieces of corrugated cardboard taped together. Tape the stacked pieces to the cardboard base.

Paint Container
Paper milk cartons (with the tops removed) stapled together and with cardboard handles make ideal containers for colored paint and water.

Paint Dispensers
Plastic mustard or ketchup containers make good paint dispensers. An aluminum nail in the top of each will keep the paint fresh. In some cases, the plastic containers can be used for painting directly from the container. Syrup pitchers make good paint dispensers and are ideal for storing paint.

Plastic Spoons
Keep plastic spoons in cans of powdered tempera for easy paint dispensing.

(From Mayesky, Mary. *Creative Activites for Young Children*, 7th ed., Clifton Park, NY: Delmar Learning.)

- Wipe paint sets clean with paper towels. Store the sets in a cardboard carton.
- For tempera paint or watercolor, rinse brushes in clean water, blot, gently point bristles, and leave to dry standing upright in a container.
- Clean brushes after each use. Neglect causes brushes to lose their shape. Be sure to never rest a brush vertically on its bristles. Suspend it, if possible; if not, rest it on its side.

FIGURE 3 · CREATIVE BUDGETING

Painting supplies can eat up a large part of your budget. The following ideas may help your budget (and maybe your creativity, too):

1. Individual watercolor sets can be made by pouring leftover tempera paint into egg-carton cups. Set them aside to dry and harden. Use the paints with water and brushes, just as you would ordinary paint sets.

2. Paint containers must be sturdy and inexpensive. Following are some ideas for different types of paint containers:

   - Cupcake or muffin tins are excellent for painting with several colors at a time.

   - Egg cartons work well when children are painting with cotton swabs. Cut the cartons in thirds to make four-part containers, and pour small amounts of paint into each egg cup.

   - Store liquid tempera in recycled glue or dishwashing-liquid bottles. Paint can be squirted quickly and neatly into paint cups from these bottles.

   - Use baby-food jars as paint containers. Make a holder for them by cutting circles from an egg-carton lid. An empty six-pack soft-drink carton makes a great tote for baby-food jars of paint.

   - When using paint cups, make a nontipping cup holder from an empty half-gallon milk or juice carton. Cut holes along the length of the carton and pop in the cups.

   - Sponges can be good paint holders, too. Cut a hole the exact size of the paint jar or cup in the center of the sponge, then fit the jar/cup in the hole. Besides keeping paint containers upright, the sponges also catch drips.

   - Cotton-ball painting is more fun (and neater) when you clip spring-type clothespins to the cotton balls. Children use the clothespins like handles. The same clothespins can be used when printing with small sponge pieces.

(From Mayesky, Mary. *Creative Activites for Young Children*, 7th ed., Clifton Park, NY: Delmar Learning.)

- Cover unused tempera until its next use. Do not keep tempera too long, because it becomes sour smelling.

Enjoying the Painting Process

Young children naturally enjoy painting, but eager young painters may require some help learning how to:

- *Prepare paint trays for use.* With watercolor paint sets, put a drop or two of water in each paint color to moisten it. Remember to dip the brush in water to clean it before dipping it into another color.

- Use a variety of brush strokes.

- Paint directly on paper, using full, free strokes.

- Use the point, side, and flat surfaces of the brush. Try wide lines, thin lines, zigzag lines, and dots and dabs.

- Mix colors on paper.

- Dip one side of the brush in one color and the other side in a second color to blend paint in one stroke.

- Remove excess paint or water from a brush by using the side of the paint container.

- Clean paint trays with paper towels or sponges.

- Rinse brushes in water and dry them with the bristles up.

Exploring Finger Painting

Finger painting is an especially good activity for young children, because it can be done over and over again. This repetition stresses the process, not the product. This book has many finger-painting activities and recipes young children will enjoy.

For finger painting, you may purchase premixed finger paint, or you may mix powdered tempera paint with liquid starch to make your own finger paint. To make your own finger paint, pour a generous dollop of starch onto paper, then sprinkle it with dry tempera. Then, have the children mix the materials with their fingers. Some teachers like to stir the dry pigment into an entire container of liquid starch. No matter how you prepare the paint, be ready to add more ingredients as the children work. The results to strive for in mixing are rich, brilliant color and sufficient paint to fill the paper when the children wish. Children must also be allowed to experiment with the paint, using their fingers, the palms of their hands, their wrists, and their arms. The children may enjoy helping to mix a recipe from **Figure 4**, which tells how to make additional kinds of finger paint.

Remember that some children dislike the feel of finger paint. Never force these children to use finger paint. Instead, substitute painting with a brush.

Now enter the world of painting. Enjoy the trip!

FIGURE 4 · FINGER-PAINT RECIPES*

Starch and Soap Finger Paint

1 cup starch
1-1/2 cups boiling water
1/2 cup soap flakes (not soap powder)
1 tablespoon glycerine (optional, makes it smoother)

Method: Mix the starch with enough water to make a smooth paste. Add the boiling water, and cook until glossy. Stir in the soap flakes while the mixture is warm. When the mixture is cool, add glycerine and coloring (powder paint, poster paint, or vegetable coloring).

Flour and Salt Finger Paint, Cooked

2 cups flour
2 teaspoons salt
3 cups cold water
2 cups hot water

Method: Add the salt to the flour, then pour the mixture into the cold water gradually. Beat the mixture with an egg beater until the mixture is smooth. Add the hot water and boil until the mixture becomes glossy. Beat the mixture until smooth, then mix in the coloring.

Flour and Salt Finger Paint, Uncooked

1 cup flour
1-1/2 teaspoons salt
1 cup water

Method: Combine the flour and salt, then add the water. This mixture has a grainy quality, unlike other finger paints, providing a different sensory experience.

Argo™ Starch Finger Paint

1/2 cup boiling water
2 tablespoons Argo starch
6 tablespoons cold water

Method: Dissolve the starch in cold water in a cup. Add this mixture to the boiling water, stirring constantly. Heat the mixture until it becomes glossy. Add color.

Wheat Flour Finger Paint

3 parts water
1 part wheat flour

Method: Stir the flour into the water, and add food coloring. (Wheat flour can be bought at low cost in wallpaper or department stores.)

Tempera Finger Paint

Dry tempera paint
1/2 cup liquid starch or
1/2 cup liquid dishwashing detergent

Method: Mix the tempera paint with the starch or detergent, adding the starch gradually until the desired thickness is reached. Paint extender can also be added to dry tempera paint.

*Interesting smells can be obtained by adding different food flavorings (e.g., mint, cloves) or talcum powder to the finger paint, if desired.

(From Mayesky, Mary. *Creative Activites for Young Children*, 7th ed., Clifton Park, NY: Delmar Learning.)

5
Years Old and Up

Accordion Painting

MATERIALS

☐ construction paper
☐ tempera paint
☐ brushes

HELPFUL HINTS

• This activity is appropriate for children with good, small motor development, because folding requires small motor skill in the fingers and hands.

• If you do this activity with younger children, you will need to fold the papers for them before they do the painting.

DEVELOPMENTAL GOALS

Develop creativity, small motor development, and hand-eye coordination and explore a new painting technique that practices paper folding.

PREPARATION

Practice with the children on how to accordion pleat the paper by folding it back and forth until the entire paper is folded.

PROCESS

1. Paint a picture or design on the construction paper.
2. Let the picture/design dry thoroughly.
3. Accordion pleat the painting.
4. This gives an interesting three-dimensional effect.

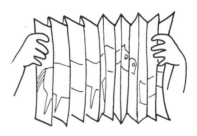

VARIATIONS

• Accordion pleat the paper before painting on it. This produces another interesting effect.
• Accordion pleat a finger painting or crayon or marker drawing.

NOTES FOR NEXT TIME: _____

_____

_____

_____

Baby-Oil Painting

MATERIALS

- [ ] any color bond (copy) paper
- [ ] cotton balls/ Q-Tips© or cotton swabs
- [ ] paintbrush
- [ ] baby oil

HELPFUL HINT

- This activity works best on bond (copy) paper, because the baby oil quickly absorbs into it.

DEVELOPMENTAL GOALS

Develop creativity, small motor development, and hand-eye coordination and explore a new material for painting.

PREPARATION

Pour a small amount of baby oil into a shallow bowl for each child. Cover the work area with a newspaper.

PROCESS

1. Dip the cotton ball in the baby oil.
2. Draw on the paper with the cotton ball.
3. Dip the cotton swab or paintbrush in the baby oil and draw some more.
4. After it soaks in, lift the picture to the light to see the work of art.

VARIATION

- Use eyedroppers to draw with the baby oil.

NOTES FOR NEXT TIME: _____

_____

_____

_____

Bag Finger Painting

MATERIALS

☐ large sealable storage bags

☐ liquid starch

☐ tempera paint

HELPFUL HINT

- Let the children who are able to help prepare the Ziploc© bags. It will save you time and they will love doing it!

DEVELOPMENTAL GOALS

Develop creativity, small motor development, and hand-eye coordination and explore a new way to mix colors.

PREPARATION

Put a small amount of liquid starch and a small amount of dry tempera paint inside the bag. Give each child one of the sealable storage bags.

PROCESS

1. Using the fingertips (no nails!), make a design on the bag.
2. Colors emerge as fingers move and mix the tempera into the liquid starch.

VARIATIONS

- Add two primary colors of dry tempera paint. Watch the colors mix!
- After mixing the paint, open the bag and squeeze it onto paper. Then, use a brush to make designs on the paper.

NOTES FOR NEXT TIME: _____

_____

_____

_____

_____

5 Years Old and UP

Batik Painting

MATERIALS

- ☐ paper
- ☐ crayons
- ☐ tempera paint
- ☐ brushes
- ☐ shallow container with water in it (a dishpan works well)
- ☐ paper towels

HELPFUL HINTS

- Dark paints make the most striking effects in batik activities.
- Bring in some batik cloth for the children to compare to their paintings. You will find batik cloth in a fabric store with the cotton fabrics.

DEVELOPMENTAL GOALS

Develop creativity, small motor development, and hand-eye coordination and explore a batik-painting technique.

PREPARATION

Dilute the tempera paint to a watery consistency.

PROCESS

1. Make a crayon drawing or design on paper.
2. Soak the paper in water.
3. Crumble the paper into a ball.
4. Uncrumble and flatten the paper.
5. Blot off the excess water with a paper towel.
6. Flow a diluted tempera paint over the surface with a brush.
7. Because the color will be more intense in the creased area, the finished drawing will have dramatic contrasts.

VARIATION

- Use different kinds of paper for the crayon drawings, such as brown paper bags, wrapping paper, and newspaper.

NOTES FOR NEXT TIME: _____

_____

_____

_____

Blow Painting

All Ages

MATERIALS

☐ typing or copy paper

☐ watery tempera in small containers

☐ plastic spoons

☐ straws

HELPFUL HINT

• An adult will have to spoon the tempera paint onto the paper for very young children.

DEVELOPMENTAL GOALS

Develop creativity, small motor development, and hand-eye coordination and explore a new painting technique.

PREPARATION

Give each child a small amount of watery tempera paint in a container and a plastic spoon.

PROCESS

1. Spoon a very small puddle of tempera onto the paper.
2. Use the straw to blow the paint in various directions, creating a variety of patterns.
3. Blow gently, hard, and so forth.

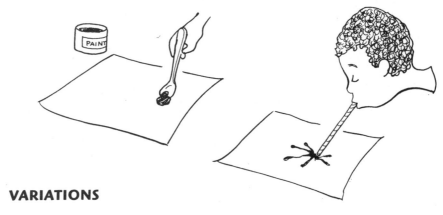

VARIATIONS

• Go outside and enjoy blow painting as the real wind blows!
• After the painting dries, add details with crayons and markers.
• Add a second color of tempera paint and blow paint on the same sheet of paper.

NOTES FOR NEXT TIME: _____

_____

_____

_____

_____

Bubble Painting

MATERIALS

- ☐ 2/3 cup liquid detergent
- ☐ gallon container
- ☐ food coloring
- ☐ tempera paint
- ☐ paper towels
- ☐ straws or bubble pipes

HELPFUL HINT

- Be sure to blow into the straws— You do not want children to drink "soap soup." Poke a small hole at the top of the straw to prevent accidental sipping.

DEVELOPMENTAL GOALS

Develop creativity, small motor development, and hand-eye coordination and explore a new painting technique that uses a familiar substance in a new way.

PREPARATION

Make a bubble solution by pouring 2/3 cup of liquid detergent into a gallon container. Add 1 tablespoon food coloring and enough water to fill the container. Let the solution sit for a few hours before using. Put the solution in clear plastic containers, and add liquid food coloring or tempera paint in primary colors.

PROCESS

1. Form secondary colors by mixing different food colors into primary colors. For example, place yellow food coloring in the red bubble solution to make orange.
2. Blow bubbles with straws.
3. Compare the bubbles made with these colored solutions to bubbles made with plain solution.
4. Blow colored bubbles over a paper towel.
5. Interesting spatter designs will result when the bubbles burst.

VARIATION

- Prepare a dark bubble solution. Place it in a cereal bowl. Blow bubbles with a straw until they fill the bowl, reaching barely above the edge of the bowl. Carefully place a light sheet of construction paper over the top of the bowl. Bubbles will pop on the paper and leave a circular design.

NOTES FOR NEXT TIME: _____

_____

_____

_____

_____

Cardboard-Brush Painting

MATERIALS

- ☐ tempera paint in small shallow containers
- ☐ pieces of cardboard of varying lengths and widths
- ☐ paper

HELPFUL HINT

- Older children can help cut the cardboard into different widths and lengths.

DEVELOPMENTAL GOALS

Develop creativity, small motor development, and hand-eye coordination and explore a new use for cardboard.

PREPARATION

Give each child several pieces of cardboard of different lengths and widths.

PROCESS

1. Dip the piece of cardboard into the tempera paint.
2. Draw a picture or design using the cardboard as a brush.
3. Bend the top of the cardboard, dip it in paint, and dab it onto the picture.
4. Make wide lines, thin lines, zigzag lines, and dots and dabs.

VARIATIONS

- Mix colors on the page with the cardboard brush.
- Include white tempera paint with paint of primary colors. Watch how the colors change!

NOTES FOR NEXT TIME: _____

_____

_____

_____

_____

A

Chocolate-Pudding Finger Painting

MATERIALS

☐ package of instant chocolate pudding

☐ wax paper

HELPFUL HINTS

• This is a good activity for very young children who put everything in their mouths.

The only problem is that they might try to taste all the finger paint! Be watchful of this possibility.

• This is an excellent activity for creative expression, because it does not involve a permanent product. The process is the focus of this activity.

DEVELOPMENTAL GOALS

Develop creativity, small motor development, and hand-eye coordination and explore a new finger painting material.

PREPARATION

Mix the instant chocolate pudding according to the directions on the package.

PROCESS

1. Give each child a piece of wax paper.
2. Put a tablespoon or more of chocolate pudding on the wax paper.
3. Have the child finger paint with the chocolate pudding on the wax paper.

VARIATION

• Add mint flavoring to the pudding for an interesting smell and taste!

NOTES FOR NEXT TIME: _____

_____

_____

_____

All Ages

Cold-Cream Finger Painting

MATERIALS

- ☐ any brand of cold cream
- ☐ dry tempera paint
- ☐ paper
- ☐ shallow dishes

HELPFUL HINTS

- This is good for a first experience with a child reluctant to use colored paint with the fingers.

- Let the children mix the dry tempera into the cold cream. It is fun to see how the color mixes in and changes the cold cream's color. In addition, it is a good activity for the small muscles in the fingers and hands.

- Be aware of any allergies to the cream or ingredients in the cream.

DEVELOPMENTAL GOALS

Develop creativity, small motor development, and hand-eye coordination and explore a new material for finger painting.

PREPARATION

Divide the cold cream into separate shallow dishes.

PROCESS

1. Spoon dry tempera into the cold cream and mix.
2. Keep adding and mixing dry tempera until you get the desired color.
3. Finger paint on the paper with the colored cold cream.

VARIATIONS

- Mix two colors of dry tempera into the cold cream and watch the colors mix.
- Finger paint directly on the tabletop with the colored cold cream. Make a print from the finger painting.

NOTES FOR NEXT TIME: _____

_____

_____

_____

_____

Comb Painting

MATERIALS

- ☐ plastic combs of different sizes
- ☐ tempera paint
- ☐ brushes
- ☐ paper

HELPFUL HINT

- If you lack combs, a piece of notched cardboard will give similar results when drawn through the wet paint.

DEVELOPMENTAL GOALS

Develop creativity, small motor development, and hand-eye coordination and explore a new painting technique that uses recycled combs.

PREPARATION

Give each child several combs of different sizes.

PROCESS

1. The child makes a picture or design on paper with tempera paint.
2. Draw the comb(s) through the wet paint.
3. Make jabs, lines, and zigzags with the comb in the wet paint.

VARIATIONS

- Make a finger painting on paper. Draw combs through the wet finger paint.
- Use an old toothbrush or hairbrush and draw it through the wet paint.

NOTES FOR NEXT TIME: _____

_____

_____

_____

_____

Cotton-Ball Painting

MATERIALS

☐ cotton balls

☐ tempera paint in shallow containers

☐ paper

HELPFUL HINTS

- For children who dislike getting paint on their fingers, use a clothespin to hold the cotton ball.

- This is an excellent activity for very young children just beginning to paint.

DEVELOPMENTAL GOALS

Develop creativity, small motor development, and hand-eye coordination and explore a new painting technique that uses cotton balls in a new way.

PREPARATION

Give each child several cotton balls.

PROCESS

1. Dip a cotton ball in a shallow dish of tempera paint.
2. Smear or squish the cotton ball on paper.
3. Dip another cotton ball in another color.
4. Repeat the process.

VARIATIONS

- Dip a cotton ball in dry powdered paint. Rub it across dry paper to create an interesting, soft effect.

- Use different kinds of papers, such as construction paper, wallpaper scraps, or cardboard.

NOTES FOR NEXT TIME: _____

_____

_____

_____

_____

Crayon-Resist Painting

MATERIALS

- ☐ crayons
- ☐ paper
- ☐ tempera paint
- ☐ brushes

HELPFUL HINTS

- Dark paints work best for crayon resist. The dark color fills all the areas the crayon has not covered.

- Crayon resist gives the feeling of a night picture. It thrills the child to see the changes that come when the paint crosses the paper.

DEVELOPMENTAL GOALS

Develop creativity, small motor development, and hand-eye coordination and explore a crayon-and-painting technique.

PREPARATION

Thin the tempera paint so it is watery.

PROCESS

1. Draw a picture or a design on the paper with crayons, pressing hard.
2. Paint over and around the crayon drawing with the thinned tempera.
3. In the areas covered with crayon, the crayon "resists," or is not covered by the paint.

VARIATIONS

- Use a piece of white cardboard from an old gift box instead of paper.
- Use a white paper plate for the crayon drawing.

NOTES FOR NEXT TIME: _____

_____

_____

_____

4

Years Old and Up

Crayons and Tempera Paint Washing

MATERIALS

- ☐ crayons
- ☐ construction paper
- ☐ tempera paint
- ☐ brushes

HELPFUL HINTS

- Children will need to press hard with their crayon for their drawings to show through the paint.

- This is a good activity to develop cooperation between children in art activities.

DEVELOPMENTAL GOALS

Develop creativity, small motor development, and hand-eye coordination and explore a new use for crayons and tempera paint.

PREPARATION

Mix water into dry tempera until it is a watery consistency. This watery paint is a "tempera wash."

PROCESS

1. Have the child draw a picture on a colored sheet of construction paper with the same color of crayon. The crayon drawing will be hard to see.

2. Exchange the drawing with a friend.

3. The friend paints over it with the thin tempera paint in the same color as the crayon.

4. This results in a translucent piece of artwork.

VARIATIONS

- Use two colors of crayons and one color of tempera paint.
- Let the same child who colors with the crayon do the tempera paint wash.

NOTES FOR NEXT TIME: _____

_____

_____

_____

_____

Dipping It!

MATERIALS

- [ ] two or three thin tempera paints in bright colors
- [ ] shallow containers
- [ ] white paper napkins or white paper towels

HELPFUL HINTS

- Young children will need help folding the napkins or paper towels.
- These "tie-dyed" napkins can be used for various things, such as borders for bulletin boards or pictures, basket linings, and wrapping paper.

DEVELOPMENTAL GOALS

Develop creativity, small motor development, and hand-eye coordination and explore a new painting technique with paper.

PREPARATION

Put the paint in small containers, about 1 to 1-1/2" deep.

PROCESS

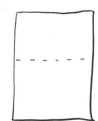

1. Give each child a white napkin or a sheet torn from a roll of white paper towels.
2. Fold the sheet in half twice.
3. Dip the corners of the napkin or towel into different colors of paint.
4. Open the napkins or towels and allow them to dry.
5. They dry into multicolored, bright designs.

VARIATIONS

- Dip the same corner into two different colors. Watch the colors blend.
- Refold the dried napkin and redip it into different colors.

NOTES FOR NEXT TIME: _____

_____

_____

_____

_____

3

Years Old and Up

Dragged Abstracts

MATERIALS

- ☐ three colors of tempera paint
- ☐ finger paint paper or white freezer paper

HELPFUL HINTS

- These abstract paintings make great wrapping paper for child-made gifts.
- This is a good activity for mixing primary colors into secondary colors. Be sure to talk about how the colors mix as the children are doing the activity.

DEVELOPMENTAL GOALS

Develop creativity, small motor development, and hand-eye coordination and explore a new technique for mixing color.

PREPARATION

On a smooth surface, counter top, linoleum, or oilcloth, put small dabs of three colors of paint. About a half teaspoon is enough of each color.

PROCESS

1. Wet the paper over a sink.
2. Let it drip.
3. Lay the paper over the paint.
4. Wiggle and twist the paper back and forth until most of it is covered. See how the colors change!
5. Lay the paintings on newspapers to dry.

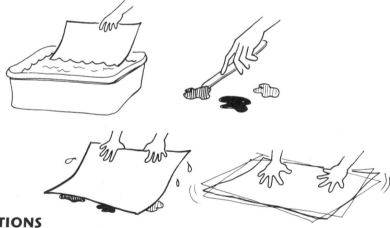

VARIATIONS

- Mix glitter with the tempera paint for an interesting effect.
- Move the paper back and forth with the feet. It is silly and fun!

NOTES FOR NEXT TIME: _____

_____

_____

_____

Copyright © 2004, Delmar Learning

PAINTING 15

Eye-Dropper Painting

MATERIALS

- ☐ eye droppers
- ☐ tempera paint
- ☐ paper

HELPFUL HINT

- This activity is appropriate for children whose small motor development allows them to hold and manipulate an eyedropper.

DEVELOPMENTAL GOALS

Develop creativity, small motor development, and hand-eye coordination and explore using eye droppers for painting.

PREPARATION

Water down the tempera paint until it is very thin. Pour the paint into small containers. Put at least one eyedropper in each container.

PROCESS

1. Using the eyedropper, drop colors of paint onto the paper.
2. Drop colors over each other and watch them mix.
3. Pull the eyedropper across the paper, squeezing color onto the paper.

VARIATIONS

- Drop paint onto wet paper with the eyedropper for a different effect.
- Use food coloring instead of tempera paint.
- Drop paint onto a coffee filter for a tie-dyed effect.

NOTES FOR NEXT TIME: _____

_____

_____

_____

All Ages

Finger Painting on Tabletops

MATERIALS

- ☐ finger paint
- ☐ Formica tabletop, an enamel-topped table, or linoleum
- ☐ newsprint paper

HELPFUL HINT

- This is a good way to save on the cost of finger paint paper and to try something new and fun, too!

DEVELOPMENTAL GOALS

Develop creativity, small motor development, and hand-eye coordination and explore a new way of finger painting.

PREPARATION

Mix the finger paints to a thick consistency.

PROCESS

1. Put a dollop of finger paint directly onto the tabletop.
2. Have the child finger paint directly onto the chosen surface.
3. Lay a piece of newsprint paper on the finger painting.
4. Gently rub the paper with one hand.
5. Finger painting is transferred from the tabletop to the paper.

VARIATION

- Use several colors of finger paint and watch the colors mix!

NOTES FOR NEXT TIME: _____

_____

_____

_____

_____

Finger Painting on Wax Paper

MATERIALS

☐ wax paper

☐ liquid dishwashing detergent

☐ dark-colored tempera paint

HELPFUL HINT

• This is a good activity to emphasize process over product. Let the children enjoy the finger paint-ing. When they are done, throw away the wax paper.

DEVELOPMENTAL GOALS

Develop creativity, small motor development, and hand-eye coordination and explore a new use for wax paper while learning a new finger-painting technique.

PREPARATION

Mix one part paint to one part soap. Give each child a generous supply of paint on individual pieces of wax paper.

PROCESS

1. Spread the dark-colored paint all over the wax paper to cover the sheet entirely.

2. Make finger-paint designs over and over on the wax paper.

3. The finger painting will have a translucent quality on the wax paper.

VARIATIONS

• Have the children help prepare the finger paint. It may be a bit messy for you, but it will be fun for the children!

• Use one long sheet of wax paper for a group finger-painting activity.

NOTES FOR NEXT TIME: _____

_____

_____

_____

_____

Finger Painting Over Crayon

MATERIALS

- ☐ paper
- ☐ liquid starch
- ☐ powdered tempera
- ☐ crayons
- ☐ brushes

HELPFUL HINT

- Press hard when making the crayon drawing. This way the drawing will show better under the finger painting.

DEVELOPMENTAL GOALS

Develop creativity, small motor development, and hand-eye coordination and explore the use of crayons and finger paint.

PREPARATION

Put liquid starch in shallow containers.

PROCESS

1. Cover the paper with brightly colored crayon designs or pictures.
2. Lay the crayoned paper on a smooth, flat surface.
3. Spread liquid starch over the crayoned picture.
4. Sprinkle a small amount of tempera paint in the liquid starch.
5. Be sure that its color contrasts with the crayon color(s).
6. Finger paint over the crayon drawing.
7. The color will mix as soon as the hand is drawn over the surface.

VARIATIONS

- Use two colors of dry tempera, such as red and yellow. Watch how it mixes to orange! Do the same with other primary colors.
- Add details by pasting bits of paper cut in shapes onto the artwork.
- Have one child do the crayon drawing and another do the finger painting.

NOTES FOR NEXT TIME: _____

_____

_____

Finger Painting with Shaving Cream

MATERIALS

- ☐ aerosol can of shaving cream
- ☐ washable tabletop or other washable surface
- ☐ dry tempera paint

HELPFUL HINT

- Be watchful for children who put everything in their mouths. Shaving cream doesn't taste very good!! For this reason, this activity is most appropriate for children past that stage.

DEVELOPMENTAL GOALS

Develop creativity, small motor development, and hand-eye coordination and explore a new material for finger painting.

PREPARATION

Be sure the paint surface is washable.

PROCESS

1. Give each child a big glob of shaving cream.
2. Finger paint with the shaving cream directly on the tabletop surface.
3. Sprinkle dry tempera paint into the shaving cream.
4. Mix the paint into the shaving cream with the fingers.

VARIATION

- Add spices for different smells, such as cinnamon or nutmeg.

NOTES FOR NEXT TIME: _____

_____

_____

_____

Flour-and-Water Painting

MATERIALS

- ☐ flour
- ☐ water
- ☐ plastic squeeze bottles (the kind honey is sold in)
- ☐ Styrofoam or aluminum pans
- ☐ construction paper
- ☐ tempera paint or food coloring
- ☐ Popsicle sticks

HELPFUL HINTS

- Be sure to test the plastic bottles for smooth flowing before beginning this activity. A stopped-up squeeze bottle can get in the way of a child's creative expression.
- Add more water to the flour mixture if the squeeze bottle gets "stuck" in the middle of the activity. Just add water and shake it to mix it in.

DEVELOPMENTAL GOALS

Develop creativity, small motor development, and hand-eye coordination and explore a new use for flour and water while learning a new painting technique.

PREPARATION

Mix one part flour with one part water. Add food coloring or tempera paint for coloring or leave the mixture white. Fill the plastic bottle halfway.

PROCESS

1. Have the child squeeze the flour mixture from the bottle, making designs on the construction paper.
2. Use a Popsicle stick to make more designs.
3. After the flour mixture dries, add more details with crayons and markers.

VARIATIONS

- Sprinkle wet designs with glitter for a sparkling effect.
- Bits of grass, leaves, or even feathers can be added before the flour mixture dries.

NOTES FOR NEXT TIME: _____

_____

_____

_____

_____

Fold-Over Painting

MATERIALS

- ☐ construction paper or any other heavy-duty paper
- ☐ tempera paint in several colors
- ☐ plastic spoons
- ☐ small shallow containers

HELPFUL HINT

- This is a good activity for young children just beginning to use paints. Using the spoon with paint is easier than using a paint-brush for some children.

DEVELOPMENTAL GOALS

Develop creativity, small motor development, and hand-eye coordination and explore new painting technique that practices folding and making two images.

PREPARATION

Mix several colors of tempera paint and put them in shallow containers.

PROCESS

1. Give each child a plastic spoon and container(s) of tempera paint.
2. Fold the paper in half.
3. Drop small dots of paint onto one side.
4. Fold the paper.
5. Gently smooth hands over the paper.
6. Open the paper and the blotted halves will form a surprise picture.

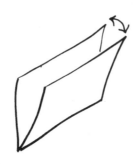

VARIATIONS

- Use two or more colors for a color mixing experience.
- Use an eyedropper instead of a spoon to drop color onto the paper.

NOTES FOR NEXT TIME: _____

_____

_____

A

All Ages

Hide-and-Seek Painting

MATERIALS

- ☐ paper
- ☐ brushes
- ☐ paint
- ☐ blindfold

HELPFUL HINT

- Not all children like to be blindfolded. Never force a child to cover the eyes for this activity or any other.

DEVELOPMENTAL GOALS

Develop creativity, small motor development, and hand-eye coordination and explore a new painting technique.

PREPARATION

Tie a blindfold over the children's eyes.

PROCESS

1. Allow the child to feel the brushes, paper, and area before starting.
2. The child paints without seeing what the child is doing.
3. Take off the blindfold and view the artwork.

VARIATIONS:

- Play music while the children are painting blindfolded.
- Read a story or poem before or while they are painting.

NOTES FOR NEXT TIME: _____

_____

_____

_____

_____

Ice-Cube Painting

MATERIALS

- ☐ ice-cube trays
- ☐ Popsicle sticks
- ☐ dry tempera paint
- ☐ finger paint paper

HELPFUL HINTS

- This is a messy activity. Be sure to cover the work area and the children well!

- This activity provides a great opportunity to talk about freezing, melting, warm air, cold air, and many other science concepts.

DEVELOPMENTAL GOALS

Develop creativity, small motor development, and hand-eye coordination and explore a new painting technique that ties science to art activities.

PREPARATION

Fill the ice-cube trays with water. Insert a Popsicle stick into each hole. Make one for each child. Let the water freeze.

PROCESS

1. Give each child a sheet of finger-paint paper. (Any glossy paper will work.)
2. Sprinkle dry tempera onto the paper.
3. Have the child rub an ice cube over the paint.
4. Watch the ice melt into color!

VARIATIONS

- Use two primary colors of dry tempera. Watch the colors mix!
- If you live in a cold climate, let the ice cubes freeze outside. Children love checking on the progress of the freezing!

NOTES FOR NEXT TIME: _____

_____

_____

_____

_____

Leaf Painting

MATERIALS

- ☐ leaves of different shapes
- ☐ tempera paint
- ☐ crayons
- ☐ markers
- ☐ tag board or heavy construction paper
- ☐ small stones

HELPFUL HINTS

- Gather the small stones on the same walk you take for gathering the leaves for this activity.
- This is a good activity to use the painted backpacks made in the "Making Painted Backpacks" activity of this book.

DEVELOPMENTAL GOALS

Develop creativity, small motor development, and hand-eye coordination and explore a new painting technique that ties science to art activities.

PREPARATION

Go outside and collect a supply of fallen leaves. If possible, collect bright fall-colored leaves. Fallen leaves that are not fall colored will work as well. Talk about the leaves—their shapes, their sizes, their colors, their lines.

PROCESS

1. Have the child choose a leaf for its color and/or shape.
2. Place the leaf on a piece of heavy construction or tag board.
3. Hold the leaf down with a small stone.
4. Paint around the outline of the leaf.
5. Choose another leaf and repeat the process until the paper is filled.
6. When the paint is dry, remove the stones to see the leaf's outline.

VARIATIONS

- Use crayons or markers to trace the leaf outline.
- Older children may want to label the leaf. Have the children look up the leaves they cannot identify.

NOTES FOR NEXT TIME: _____

_____

_____

_____

_____

Making Painted Backpacks

MATERIALS

- [ ] large, empty detergent boxes
- [ ] scissors
- [ ] construction paper
- [ ] paste
- [ ] tempera paint
- [ ] crayons
- [ ] markers
- [ ] heavy, soft yarn

HELPFUL HINTS

- Children can carry their favorite toys, dolls, and stuffed animals in their backpacks.

- These backpacks are great to take along on an outdoor walk for storing nature's treasures found along the way!

- Ask parents and friends to save detergent boxes for this activity.

DEVELOPMENTAL GOALS

Develop creativity, small motor development, and hand-eye coordination and create a useful object from recycled materials.

PREPARATION

Cut the top off the detergent box. Punch holes to string the heavy, soft yarn through the box.

PROCESS

1. Paste a piece of construction paper on the front of the box.

2. Paint a picture or design on the construction paper.

3. Add more details with crayons or markers after the paint has dried.

4. Loop the yarn through the holes in the box.

5. Try on the backpack and adjust the yarn so the backpack comfortably fits the child.

VARIATIONS

- Make detergent box totes with the yarn at both sides of the top of the box.

- Paint the child's name in large print on the backpack. Let it dry. Then, have the child decorate around his or her name. Wearing these on an outdoor walk is a good way to keep up with the children!

NOTES FOR NEXT TIME: _____

_____

_____

_____

4

Years Old and Up

Making Stand-Up Painted Faces

MATERIALS

- ☐ construction paper
- ☐ paste or tape
- ☐ tempera paint
- ☐ brushes
- ☐ bits of cloth or trim
- ☐ scraps of wrapping or wallpaper
- ☐ yarn

HELPFUL HINTS

- Encourage the children to use as many facial details as possible. Some suggestions are eyes, nose, mouth, teeth, glasses, freckles, cheeks, ears, hair, and mustache.
- Remember to paint the back of the head, too!

DEVELOPMENTAL GOALS

Develop creativity, small motor development, and hand-eye coordination and create painted objects using paper.

PREPARATION

Roll a piece of paper to form a cylinder. Paper 12" × 12" works best. Paste or tape the edges. If using paste, press from the inside to make the paste hold securely. If using tape, tape on the inside of the cylinder.

PROCESS

1. Stand the cylinder on end.
2. Paint facial details on the cylinder.
3. Add clothing details with bits of construction paper, fabric or trim scraps, bits of wallpaper, or wrapping paper.

VARIATIONS

- Make stand-up animals.
- Older children enjoy making stand-up faces of favorite storybook characters.

NOTES FOR NEXT TIME: _____

_____

_____

_____

_____

Marble Painting

MATERIALS

- ☐ marbles
- ☐ paper
- ☐ scissors
- ☐ tempera paint in several colors
- ☐ round pan (a cake pan works well)

HELPFUL HINTS

- Picking up the marbles and dipping them in paint will leave paint on the children's fingers. To make clean up a bit easier, mix a bit of liquid detergent into the tempera paint. Washing will be soapier and easier!
- Children can help cut out the round pieces of paper. Use the cake pan to trace around. Then, cut along the traced lines.
- Do not use marbles with children under age 3 as they may be a choking hazard!

DEVELOPMENTAL GOALS

Develop creativity, small motor development, and hand-eye coordination and explore a new painting technique.

PREPARATION

Cut the paper to fit into the bottom of the cake pan. Cut one for each child.

PROCESS

1. Dip the marble in the tempera paint.
2. Put the marble into the pan lined with paper.
3. Roll the marble around, making lines and squiggles of tempera paint.
4. Repeat with another color of paint.

VARIATIONS

- Use other round objects, such as ping-pong balls and beads.
- Use related colors of paint, such as red, yellow, and orange. Watch how the colors mix!
- Use different kinds of paper, such as construction paper, newsprint, newspapers, and wallpaper scraps.

NOTES FOR NEXT TIME: _____

_____

_____

_____

Newspaper Painting

MATERIALS

- ☐ sheets of newspaper
- ☐ tempera paint
- ☐ brushes

HELPFUL HINT

- The paintings will have a transparent effect and the newspaper printing will show through the paint.

DEVELOPMENTAL GOALS

Develop creativity, small motor development, and hand-eye coordination and explore a new material for brush painting using recycled newspapers.

PREPARATION

Have several colors of tempera paint, including light colors, ready.

PROCESS

1. Paint background colors using light-colored paint over the paper.
2. The printing shows through the paint.
3. Paint designs or pictures over the background color.

VARIATIONS

- Mix sawdust or salt into the paint for an interesting, rough texture.
- Add details with crayons or markers.
- Use various objects to print designs onto the newspaper painting.

NOTES FOR NEXT TIME: _____

_____

_____

_____

_____

Painting on Cardboard

MATERIALS

☐ tempera paint

☐ paintbrushes

☐ pieces of cardboard

HELPFUL HINT

• This activity might frustrate children just beginning to paint with brushes, because the paint is not easy to control on cardboard.

DEVELOPMENTAL GOALS

Develop creativity, small motor development, and hand-eye coordination and explore painting on cardboard.

PREPARATION

Tear the top layer of paper from the cardboard so the lines (ridges) are visible.

PROCESS

1. Paint a picture or design directly onto the lined side of the cardboard.
2. Watch how the paint moves into the lines.
3. Paint along the lines.
4. Paint across the lines.

VARIATIONS

• While the painting is wet, place a piece of paper over it and press. This will make a print of the painting on the paper.

• While the paint is wet, sprinkle glitter on it. It will stick to the dried paint and give it a sparkly effect.

NOTES FOR NEXT TIME: _____

_____

_____

_____

_____

Painting on Damp Paper

MATERIALS

☐ dry or liquid tempera paint
☐ paint brushes
☐ paper
☐ water container
☐ blotting material (e.g., rag, sponge, paper towel)

HELPFUL HINTS

• Damp paper tempera painting must be done hurriedly to be lively.

• Do not expect complete success on the first try. Only experience will tell just how wet the paper must be and how much paint should be used.

• Clean the brush and the water in the container often during this activity.

• This activity is not suitable for beginning painters. It is better for children who are used to painting with brushes.

DEVELOPMENTAL GOALS

Develop creativity, small motor development, and hand-eye coordination and explore a new technique for brush painting.

PREPARATION

Soak the paper thoroughly in water.

PROCESS

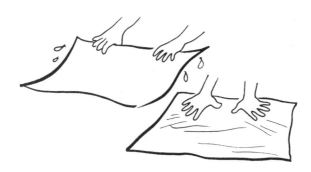

1. Lay the wet paper on the tabletop and smooth all the wrinkles.

2. Blot any pools of water with blotting material.

3. Paint directly on the damp paper.

4. Paint light colors at first, and second and third colors before the paper dries, so the colors will mingle and blend into soft shapes.

5. Details can be painted in when the painting is dry.

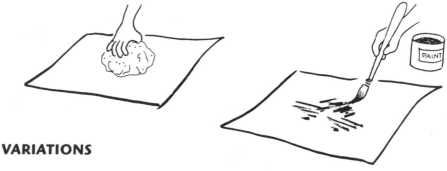

VARIATIONS

• Sprinkle glitter into the wet paint for a sparkly effect.

• Glue on bits of scrap fabric or trim for added texture.

NOTES FOR NEXT TIME: _____

_____

_____

Painting Snow Pictures with Cotton

MATERIALS

- ☐ colored construction paper
- ☐ tempera paint
- ☐ brushes
- ☐ cotton balls
- ☐ paste

HELPFUL HINTS

- White paste works best with cotton balls.
- Remind the children to dip the cotton balls in paste and to not use their fingers to apply the paste. If the children have paste on their fingers, the cotton will stick to them!

DEVELOPMENTAL GOALS

Develop creativity, small motor development, and hand-eye coordination and explore a new tool for painting.

PREPARATION

Talk about the first day of snow or just after a big storm. For those in temperate climates, talk about pictures the children have seen of snow. Discuss how snow piles up on roofs, trees, cars, and so on.

PROCESS

1. Have the child paint a picture on colored construction paper.
2. Once the painting is finished, add cotton to represent snow.
3. Roll cotton into small balls to make it look like snow falling, snowballs, or even snowmen.
4. Glue the cotton bits to the painting.

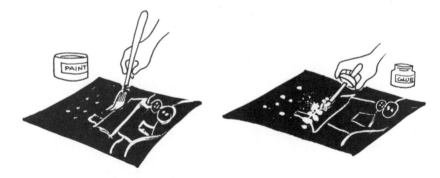

VARIATIONS

- Glue glitter to the "snow" for an interesting effect.
- Draw pictures of houses and trees and add "snow" to them.

NOTES FOR NEXT TIME: _____

_____

_____

_____

_____

Painting through Tissue

MATERIALS

- ☐ white tissue paper
- ☐ tempera paint
- ☐ brushes
- ☐ heavyweight paper or pieces of cardboard or pieces of white gift boxes

HELPFUL HINT

- This is an excellent activity for children who have a lot of experience painting with brushes.

DEVELOPMENTAL GOALS

Develop creativity, small motor development, and hand-eye coordination and explore painting on tissue paper.

PREPARATION

Soak the heavyweight paper, pieces of cardboard, or white gift boxes in water.

PROCESS

1. Lay a sheet of white tissue paper over the wet heavyweight paper.
2. Carefully apply more water to the tissue.
3. Paint the tissue.
4. Enjoy the wrinkles and "bubbled areas" that result on the tissue.
5. When the tissue painting dries, carefully remove and discard the tissue paper.
6. See how the tissue "painted" the heavyweight paper beneath the tissue.

VARIATIONS

- Brush or drop on tempera paint in related colors, such as red, yellow, and orange; yellow, blue, and green; or red, blue and purple.
- On the dried artwork, add details with colored pencils, markers, or tempera paint.

NOTES FOR NEXT TIME: _____

_____

_____

_____

_____

Painting to Music

MATERIALS

- ☐ tempera paint
- ☐ paper
- ☐ brushes
- ☐ tapes or CDs
- ☐ tape or CD player

HELPFUL HINT

- Children will enjoy taking turns choosing the music for this activity.

DEVELOPMENTAL GOALS

Develop creativity, small motor development, and hand-eye coordination and explore a new way to paint that ties music to art activities.

PREPARATION

Choose music to play while the children paint. Begin with music that has a definite beat that is easy to hear.

PROCESS

1. Play the music for the children.
2. Discuss the beat and the way the music makes the children feel or want to move.
3. Have the children paint pictures or designs while the music is playing.
4. Encourage the children to make brush strokes to "go with the music."
5. After the children are finished, talk about the paintings and how the music made them feel while they were painting.

VARIATIONS

- Finger paint to music
- Make a collage to music.
- Work with clay or play dough to music.

NOTES FOR NEXT TIME: _____

_____

_____

_____

_____

3

Years Old and Up

Painting with Weeds

MATERIALS

- ☐ tempera paint in shallow containers (e.g., aluminum pie tins)
- ☐ paper
- ☐ weeds collected outdoors

HELPFUL HINTS

- Queen Ann's lace makes an excellent paintbrush.
- In the fall, many weeds are at maximum heights and can be collected on class walks for later use in art activities.
- Wild oats and golden rod also work well for this activity. Be sure the children are not allergic to these weeds or any others used in this activity.

DEVELOPMENTAL GOALS

Develop creativity, small motor development, and hand-eye coordination and explore a new painting technique that ties nature to art activities.

PREPARATION

Mix the tempera paint and pour enough of it in the pie pan to cover the bottom. Give each child a piece of paper.

PROCESS

1. Have the child choose a weed to use as a brush.

2. Dip the weed in the paint.

3. Make a design or a picture on the paper.

VARIATIONS

- Choose another weed to use on the painting or on a new painting.
- Save the weeds used for painting to add to later collage activities.
- Let the weeds dry, and use them later in dough-sculpture designs.

NOTES FOR NEXT TIME: _____

_____

_____

_____

_____

3
Years Old and UP

Paper-Towel Painting

MATERIALS

- ☐ paper towels
- ☐ tempera paint
- ☐ shallow containers
- ☐ paper

HELPFUL HINT

- Be sure to have the children wad the paper. It is fun for them and a good small motor activity, as well!

DEVELOPMENTAL GOALS

Develop creativity, small motor development, and hand-eye coordination and explore a new painting technique that uses paper towels in a new way.

PREPARATION

Wad the paper towel into a ball.

PROCESS

1. Dip the paper towel in paint.
2. Dab, press, or rub the paper towel on the paper.
3. Dip the paper towel in another color of paint.
4. Repeat the process.

VARIATIONS

- Use other kinds of paper, such as foil, wax paper, and wallpaper scraps.
- Wad two towels. Dip in paint and paint with both hands!

NOTES FOR NEXT TIME: _____
_____
_____
_____

4
Years Old and UP

Plastic-Wrap Painting

MATERIALS

- ☐ heavy paper (e.g., cardboard, pieces of white gift boxes)
- ☐ tempera paint
- ☐ plastic wrap (the kind used in cooking)

HELPFUL HINTS

- This activity is most appropriate for children who have a good amount of experience in painting with a brush.
- The wetter the paint, the better the plastic wrap will stick to and wrinkle on the paint.

DEVELOPMENTAL GOALS

Develop creativity, small motor development, and hand-eye coordination and explore a new use for plastic wrap that teaches a new painting technique.

PREPARATION

Be ready to cut the plastic wrap when the child needs it in this activity.

PROCESS

1. Quickly paint a piece of heavy paper with tempera paint.
2. Squeeze some more drops of liquid tempera over the surface.
3. Lay a sheet of plastic wrap over the wet surface.
4. Shapes and patterns will result from the wrinkled areas.
5. When the painting is dry, remove the plastic.

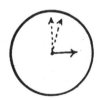

VARIATION

- Add more details to the artwork with crayons, markers, or more paint.

NOTES FOR NEXT TIME: _____

_____

_____

_____

_____

Pulled-String Painting

MATERIALS

- ☐ string
- ☐ paper
- ☐ tempera paint
- ☐ heavy cardboard or piece of board
- ☐ brushes
- ☐ sponge

HELPFUL HINT

- This activity is suitable for children who have fairly well developed small motor skills, usually ages 5 and up.

NOTES FOR NEXT TIME:

_____

_____

_____

_____

DEVELOPMENTAL GOALS

Develop creativity, small motor development, and hand-eye coordination and explore a new technique for painting.

PREPARATION

Mix the tempera paints so they are watery. Give each child several lengths of string, at least 12" long.

PROCESS

1. Place a sheet of paper on a flat surface.
2. Coat the string thoroughly with paint.
3. Arrange the paint-soaked string on the paper.
4. Twisted loops in the string make interesting effects.
5. Allow one or two ends to extend beyond the same edge of the paper.
6. Place another piece of paper over this string arrangement.
7. Cover the paper with a firm piece of cardboard or a piece of wood.
8. Hold the paper in place lightly with one hand.
9. With the other hand, grasp the ends of the string and pull it gently from between the papers.
10. Carefully peel the two papers apart. The design will be duplicated on the second sheet of paper.

VARIATIONS

- Coat the string with different colors of paint. Watch how the colors mix.
- Use different kinds of string, rope, and cording to make different sizes of lines.

Q-Tip© Painting

MATERIALS

- ☐ Q-tips© or cotton swabs
- ☐ tempera paint
- ☐ paper

HELPFUL HINTS

- This activity requires good small motor development. It is suitable for children who are familiar with brush painting.

- Have a good supply of Q-tips© on hand, so children can use as many as they want in this activity.

DEVELOPMENTAL GOALS

Develop creativity, small motor development, and hand-eye coordination and explore painting with cotton swabs.

PREPARATION

Put the tempera paint in shallow containers. Give each child at least six Q-tips©.

PROCESS

1. Have the child dip a Q-tip© into the tempera paint.
2. Draw a picture or design with the Q-tip©.
3. Make dabs, dot, zigzags, and squiggles with the Q-tip©.

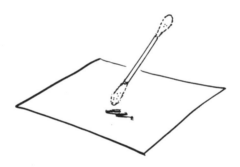

VARIATIONS

- Paint with cotton balls and Q-tips©.
- Add more details with a regular paintbrush.

NOTES FOR NEXT TIME: _____

_____

_____

_____

Salty Painting

MATERIALS

☐ paper
☐ brushes
☐ tempera paint
☐ salt

HELPFUL HINTS

- Have the children fill the various salt shakers. They will love doing this, and it is good hand-eye and small motor exercise for the children.

- Talk about the effects the salt makes on the paint. Encourage use of descriptive words like *splotchy*, *spotty*, *blobs*, and other such words.

DEVELOPMENTAL GOALS

Develop creativity, small motor development, and hand-eye coordination and explore a new painting technique that shows the effects of salt on paint.

PREPARATION

Put salt in shakers with various sizes of holes on top.

PROCESS

1. Paint a picture or design with tempera paint.
2. Sprinkle salt onto the wet tempera paint.
3. See the interesting splotches and runny spots appear.
4. Shake salt on with a shaker with a different size of holes on top.
5. See the difference in the splotches and spots.

VARIATION

- Shake salt on finger paintings.

NOTES FOR NEXT TIME: _____

_____

_____

_____

_____

Sand Painting

MATERIALS

- ☐ tempera paint
- ☐ brushes
- ☐ sand
- ☐ glue
- ☐ construction paper

HELPFUL HINT

- Sand will, of course, fall here and there during this activity. Be prepared! Cover the work area with newspapers so the sand can be scooped up after the activity is over.

DEVELOPMENTAL GOALS

Develop creativity, small motor development, and hand-eye coordination and explore using sand with painting.

PREPARATION

Put sand in separate, small, shallow containers for each child's use.

PROCESS

1. Brush glue onto the construction paper.
2. Sprinkle sand onto the glue.
3. Paint a picture or design around the sand.

VARIATION

- Paint the sand. Watch what happens!

NOTES FOR NEXT TIME: _____

_____

_____

_____

_____

Spatter Painting

MATERIALS

- ☐ construction paper
- ☐ scissors (optional)
- ☐ toothbrushes
- ☐ piece of screen
- ☐ tempera paint

HELPFUL HINTS

- This is a very messy activity, but it is worth the mess, because children are fascinated by seeing how the outline remains after the spattering is over.

- If you are using recycled toothbrushes for this activity, be sure to run them through the dishwasher or soak them in boiling water before using them with the children.

DEVELOPMENTAL GOALS

Develop creativity, small motor development, and hand-eye coordination and explore a spatter-painting technique.

PREPARATION

Cut a screen into pieces about 6 to 8" square. Put tempera paint in shallow containers (e.g., aluminum pie tins).

PROCESS

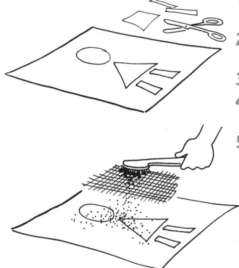

1. Have the child cut or tear a shape out of construction paper.
2. Place the shape on a background sheet of paper.
3. Dip a toothbrush in paint.
4. Rub the toothbrush over the screen.
5. When the shape is removed, its outline remains.

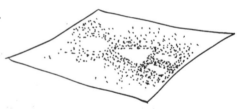

VARIATIONS

- Repeat the process using a different color of paint, placing the shape in a different place on the paper.
- Repeat the process using different shapes.
- Use natural forms, such as twigs, leaves, and grass.

NOTES FOR NEXT TIME: _____

_____

_____

_____

_____

A

All Ages

Sponge Painting

MATERIALS

- ☐ sponge cut into a variety of sizes and shapes
- ☐ scissors
- ☐ liquid tempera paint
- ☐ paper
- ☐ brushes

HELPFUL HINTS

- An adult will need to assist very young children in soaking and smoothing the paper for this activity.
- Sometimes the process of soaking and smoothing the paper is as much fun as the sponge painting! Be prepared for this.

DEVELOPMENTAL GOALS

Develop creativity, small motor development, and hand-eye coordination and explore painting with sponges.

PREPARATION

Soak the paper thoroughly in water. Moisten the sponge pieces. Put tempera paint in shallow containers (e.g., aluminum pie tins).

PROCESS

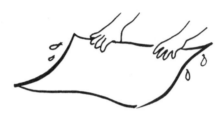

1. Lay the wet paper on a smooth surface and remove all the wrinkles and excess water.
2. Dip the sponge pieces in the tempera paint.
3. Apply the sponge to moist paper.
4. Make a picture or a design by using sponges of different shapes and sizes.
5. Allow the colors to mix and blend.

VARIATIONS

- Begin with two primary colors for younger children.
- Older children will enjoy several colors for this activity.
- Details and accents can be added with a brush when painting is dry.
- Experiment by trying this on both wet and dry paper.

NOTES FOR NEXT TIME: _____

_____

_____

Spray Painting

MATERIALS

- [ ] construction paper shapes
- [ ] white construction paper
- [ ] spray bottles
- [ ] tempera paint
- [ ] small rocks to use as weights

HELPFUL HINTS

- Plan an outdoor walk to gather the small stones to use as weights in this activity.
- Be sure you check that the spray bottle is not clogged before filling it with thinned tempera paint!

DEVELOPMENTAL GOALS

Develop creativity, small motor development, and hand-eye coordination and explore a new painting technique that shows how paint looks when sprayed.

PREPARATION

Mix a thin solution of tempera paint. Pour the paint into a plastic spray bottle. Set a small funnel on your spray bottle to make this easier to do.

PROCESS

1. Cut or tear shapes out of construction paper.
2. Arrange cut out shapes in some design over the sheet of white construction paper.
3. Weigh down the shapes with the small rocks.
4. Spray the tempera paint lightly over the shape design.
5. When the paint has dried, pick up the shapes to discover the designs left underneath.

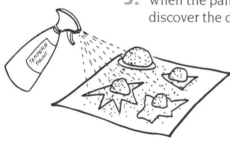

VARIATIONS

- Use crayons or markers to complete the design after the paint has dried.
- Use heavy weight washers to hold down the shapes while spraying around them.
- Very young children enjoy just spraying paint without the shapes to spray around.

NOTES FOR NEXT TIME: _____

_____

_____

Tempera and White-Glue Resist Painting

Years Old and UP

MATERIALS

- ☐ tempera paint
- ☐ paper
- ☐ white glue
- ☐ brushes
- ☐ plastic knife

HELPFUL HINT

- This activity involves waiting for the glue to dry. Very young children are not very good at waiting, so plan the first part of the activity before going outdoors. When it is time to come inside, the glue will probably be dry and the children can proceed with the rest of the activity.

DEVELOPMENTAL GOALS

Develop creativity, small motor development, and hand-eye coordination and explore a painting-resist technique.

PREPARATION

Have small brushes ready to use with the white glue. Be sure to caution the children not to use paintbrushes with the glue.

PROCESS

1. Paint a picture or design on the paper with the white glue by using the brush attached to the white glue jar or by applying with a finger.
2. Allow the glue to dry.
3. Paint over the glue picture/design with tempera paint.
4. Several colors can be mingled.
5. The glue will resist the paint.
6. Allow the paint to dry.
7. Clean away the glue with a plastic knife and expose the paper and original drawing.

VARIATION

- Glue can be painted over the areas previously painted with paint and repeated as often as desired. Make sure each is dry before applying the other.

NOTES FOR NEXT TIME: _____

_____

_____

Three-Dimensional Painting

MATERIALS

- ☐ paper
- ☐ tempera paint
- ☐ strips of construction paper
- ☐ tissue
- ☐ wrapping paper
- ☐ colored magazine paper
- ☐ glue
- ☐ scissors (optional)
- ☐ brushes

HELPFUL HINT

- You may have to demonstrate how to glue down strips to make them "bump out," but avoid doing it for the children. They will learn by experimenting with the glue and paper in the process of this activity.

DEVELOPMENTAL GOALS

Develop creativity, small motor development, and hand-eye coordination and explore a new painting technique that reinforces design texture concepts and detail placement.

PREPARATION

Talk about how strips of paper can be added to make things "bump out" or be more "three-dimensional."

PROCESS

1. Paint a picture or design on the paper.
2. Glue pieces of different kinds of paper to the picture.
3. Glue them in alternating places, making them "bump out."
4. Glue strips so they look "wavy."

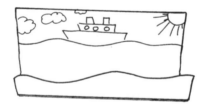

VARIATIONS

- Add other real-life objects, such as grasses, feathers, or shells.
- Glue on fabric and trim scraps for added effect.

NOTES FOR NEXT TIME: _____

_____

_____

_____

_____

Tie Dyeing

MATERIALS

- ☐ large pan of warm water
- ☐ marbles
- ☐ rubber bands
- ☐ pieces of old sheets
- ☐ undershirts, or cloth squares
- ☐ liquid tempera paint or liquid dye

HELPFUL HINTS

- If possible, do this activity outdoors to avoid spilling the dye on the floor or furniture.
- Be very watchful of children around the warm water to avoid accidents.

DEVELOPMENTAL GOALS

Develop creativity, small motor development, and hand-eye coordination and explore a new technique that uses paint as a dye.

PREPARATION

Fill a large pot one-third full of warm water. Add the liquid dye or tempera paint and stir. The brightness of the color will depend on how much dye or tempera paint you add.

PROCESS

1. Place marbles inside the cloth pieces.
2. Fasten them with a rubber band. (Adults may need to tighten the rubber bands.)
3. Tie several marbles into the cloth at different places.
4. Dip the cloth in the dye.
5. Remove the rubber bands to see that the area under the rubber band is not dyed.

VARIATIONS

- Use old, white T-shirts from home to make tie dye designs.
- Use old pillowcases.

NOTES FOR NEXT TIME: _____

_____

_____

Tissue-Dab Painting

MATERIALS

- ☐ finger paint paper or freezer paper
- ☐ tempera paint
- ☐ brushes
- ☐ facial tissue

HELPFUL HINT

- Do not let the children work at this activity so long that they start tearing the paper.

DEVELOPMENTAL GOALS

Develop creativity, small motor development, and hand-eye coordination and explore painting with tissues.

PREPARATION

Let each child wet a piece of finger paint paper or freezer paper.

PROCESS

1. Brush tempera paint over the paper quickly with a wide brush.
2. Put two colors of tempera together without stirring thoroughly.
3. Use a facial tissue to dab over the paper.
4. Take up paint randomly.
5. This provides a stippling effect, leaving light and shadowy areas.
6. Make short and curved strokes, quick dabs, or special designs.

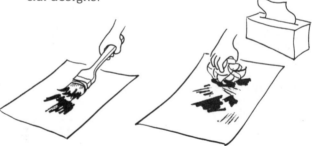

VARIATIONS

- Use bits of muslin to dab on the tempera paint. Then, let the muslin dry. The result is tie-dyed creations!
- Tissue-dab paintings make lovely wrapping paper for child-made gifts.
- They also make great bulletin-board backings.

NOTES FOR NEXT TIME: _____

_____

_____

_____

_____

Water Painting

MATERIALS

- ☐ plastic pails
- ☐ brushes of various sizes
- ☐ water

HELPFUL HINT

- This is an excellent activity for beginning painters. You need not worry about messy cleanup, and the children get the same hand-eye and small muscle exercise as using real paint.

DEVELOPMENTAL GOALS

Develop creativity, small and large motor development, and hand-eye coordination and explore a new way to paint.

PREPARATION

Locate an outside area that has many easy-to-reach surfaces the children can reach to paint.

PROCESS

1. Give the child a bucket filled with water.
2. Using a paintbrush, have the child "paint" the fence, sidewalk, and so on with water.
3. Use different sizes of paintbrushes to continue painting surfaces.

VARIATIONS

- Fill plastic spray bottles with water and "spray paint" surfaces.
- Collect paper painter's hats for the "painters" to use in this activity.

NOTES FOR NEXT TIME: _____

_____

_____

_____

_____

Wax-Paper Painting

MATERIALS

- ☐ wax paper
- ☐ heavy weight paper
- ☐ dry ballpoint pen
- ☐ Popsicle sticks
- ☐ water
- ☐ brushes
- ☐ tempera paint

HELPFUL HINT

- This activity is suitable for children who have had experience painting with brushes.

DEVELOPMENTAL GOALS

Develop creativity, small motor development, and hand-eye coordination and explore painting on wax paper.

PREPARATION

Separate the wax paper into a piece for each child.

PROCESS

1. Lay a piece of wax paper over a heavyweight sheet of paper.
2. Make designs like squiggles and loops all over with a dry ballpoint pen or Popsicle stick.
3. Press on the tool while drawing, making heavy lines.
4. Remove the wax paper.
5. Brush water over the paper's surface.
6. Immediately drop or brush on liquid paint.
7. Note that the waxy lines resist the paint.

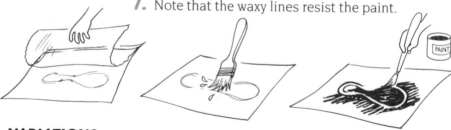

VARIATIONS

- Use more than one color paint.
- Use three related colors (e.g., red, yellow, and orange; yellow, blue, and green or red, blue and purple).
- Go back over the dried artwork with colored pencils or make designs with markers or ink in some of the small areas.

NOTES FOR NEXT TIME: _____

_____

_____

_____

Window Gardening

MATERIALS

- ☐ markers
- ☐ black crayon
- ☐ thick tempera paint in various colors
- ☐ brushes
- ☐ paper

HELPFUL HINTS

- Keep plenty of rags on hand for cleanup.
- This is a messy activity, so dress the children and cover the area accordingly, but it is worth the effort!

DEVELOPMENTAL GOALS

Develop creativity, small motor development, and hand-eye coordination and explore a new use for paint.

PREPARATION

Mix thick tempera paint in various colors with detergent so the paint sticks to the window.

PROCESS

1. Draw outlines of stems and leaves on the window(s). Make enough so each child has one flower each.
2. Work out flower pictures on paper first to get ideas for window painting.
3. Have the child use a black crayon to trace the outline on top of a stem on the window.
4. Fill the outlines with the thick tempera paint and a paintbrush.

VARIATION

- Paint bugs, birds, rainbows, and animals on the windows.

NOTES FOR NEXT TIME: _____

_____

_____

_____

Windy-Day Painting

MATERIALS

- ☐ white construction paper
- ☐ red, yellow, blue, and white dry tempera paint
- ☐ small strips of cardboard

HELPFUL HINT

- With very young children, begin with only two primary colors in this activity. As children's small motor skills improve, add more colors.

DEVELOPMENTAL GOALS

Develop creativity, small motor development, and hand-eye coordination and explore a new painting technique that ties science to art activities.

PREPARATION

Wet the white construction paper with water. Talk about the wind, how it blows, how it makes things move, how it feels on the skin, and so on.

PROCESS

1. Give each child a small amount of red, yellow, blue, and white dry tempera and several strips of cardboard.

2. Have the child use the cardboard strips to paint a windy day by quickly brushing the dry tempera onto the wet surface.

3. Encourage the children to mix and blend the colors.

VARIATIONS

- Wind motion can be used to create unusual effects with the strips. Push, pull, and twist the paint over the surface.
- Go outside and paint windy effects in the real wind!

NOTES FOR NEXT TIME: _____

_____

_____

_____

Index by Ages

ALL AGES

Bag Finger Painting 3
Blow Painting 5
Cardboard-Brush Painting 7
Chocolate-Pudding Finger Painting 8
Cold-Cream Finger Painting 9
Finger Painting on Tabletops 17
Finger Painting on Wax Paper 18
Finger Painting with Shaving Cream 20
Hide-and-Seek Painting 23
Ice-Cube Painting 24
Painting on Cardboard 30
Painting to Music 34
Sponge Painting 43
Water Painting 49

3 YEARS AND UP

Bubble Painting 6
Comb Painting 10
Cotton-Ball Painting 11
Dragged Abstracts 15
Eye-Dropper Painting 16
Finger Painting Over Crayon 19
Flour-and-Water Painting 21
Marble Painting 28
Newspaper Painting 29
Painting on Damp Paper 31
Painting Snow Pictures with Cotton 32
Painting with Weeds 35
Paper-Towel Painting 36
Q-Tip© Painting 39

Salty Painting 40
Sand Painting 41
Tissue-Dab Painting 48
Window Gardening 51
Windy-Day Painting 52

4 YEARS AND UP

Baby-Oil Painting 2
Crayon-Resist Painting 12
Crayons and Tempera Paint Washing 13
Dipping It! 14
Fold-Over Painting 22
Leaf Painting 25
Making Painted Backpacks 26
Making Stand-Up Painted Faces 27
Plastic-Wrap Painting 37
Spatter Painting 42
Spray Painting 44
Tempera and White-Glue Resist Painting . . 45
Wax-Paper Painting 50

5 YEARS AND UP

Accordion Painting 1
Batik Painting 4
Painting through Tissue 33
Pulled-String Painting 38
Three-Dimensional Painting 46
Tie Dyeing 47